ESSENTIAL ELEMENTS®

GUITAR ENSEMBLES

TOP HITS

CONTENTS

Arrangements by Chip Henderson

ISBN 978-1-4803-9660-9

HAL•LEONARD®
CORPORATION

7777 W. BLUEMOUND RD. P.O. BOX 13819 MILWAUKEE, WI 53213

Visit Hal Leonard Online at
www.halleonard.com

BLURRED LINES

Words and Music by Pharrell Williams and Robin Thicke

Chorus

D.S. al Coda
(take repeat)

Coda

GET LUCKY

Words and Music by Thomas Bangalter, Guy Manuel Homem Christo, Pharrell Williams and Nile Rodgers

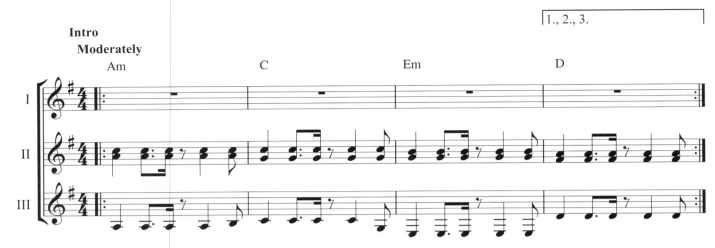

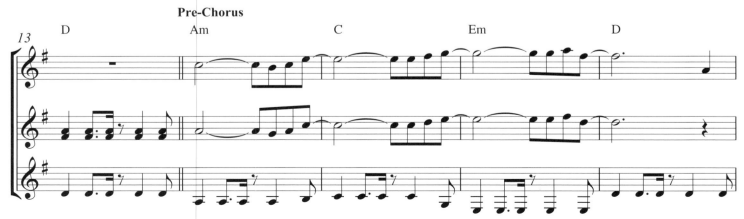

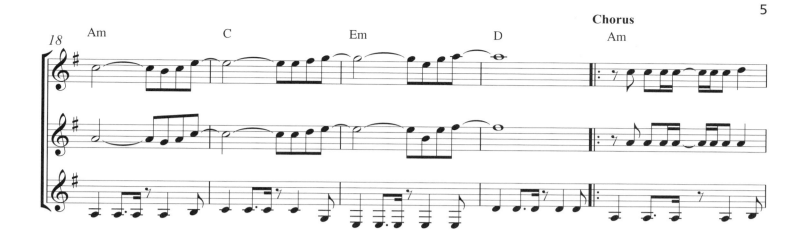

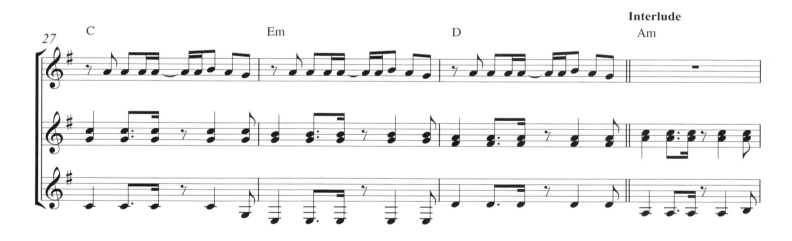

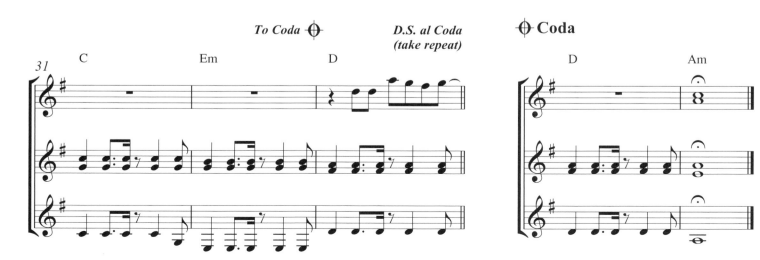

HAPPY
from DESPICABLE ME 2
Words and Music by Pharrell Williams

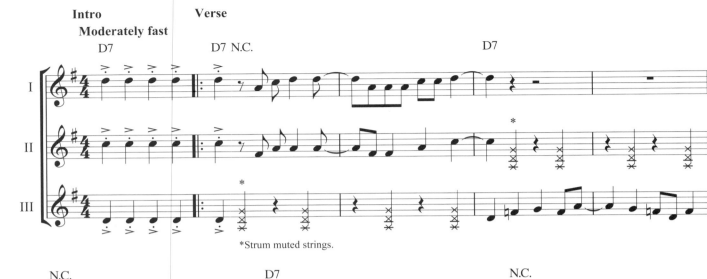

*Strum muted strings.

HO HEY

Words and Music by Jeremy Fraites and Wesley Schultz

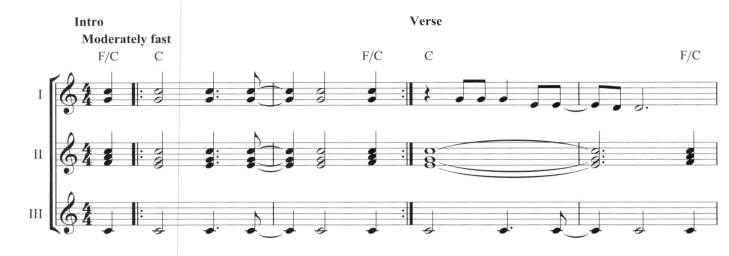

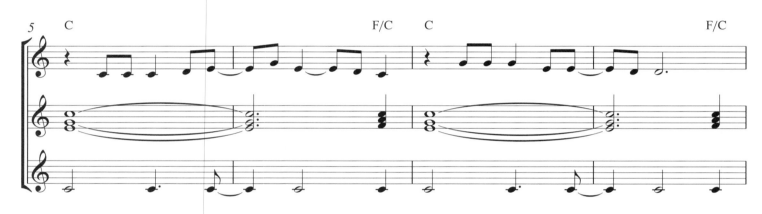

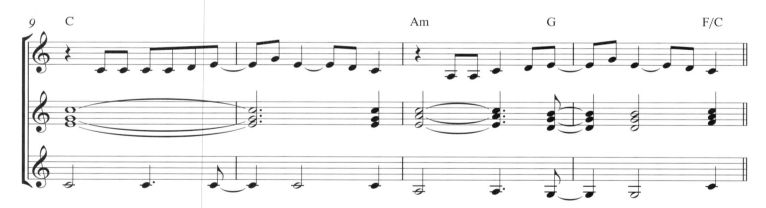

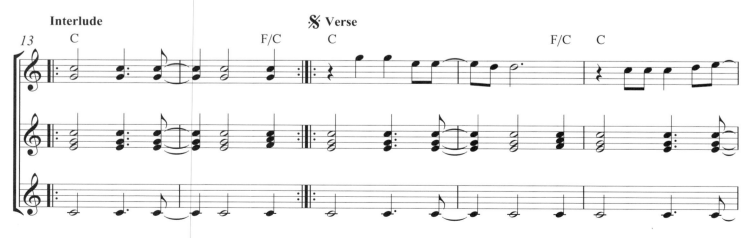

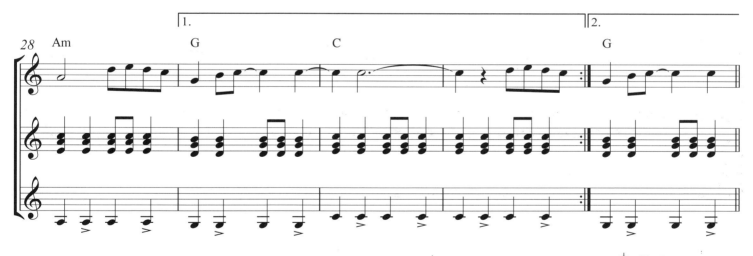

To Coda ⊕   *D.S. al Coda*
    (take repeats)   ⊕ **Coda**

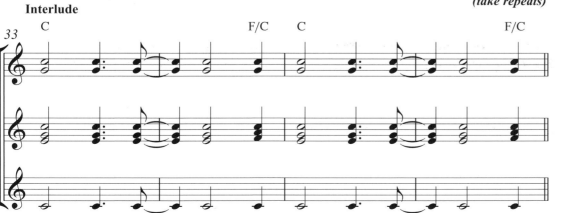

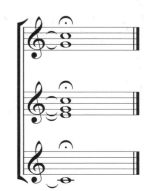

HOME

Words and Music by Greg Holden and Drew Pearson

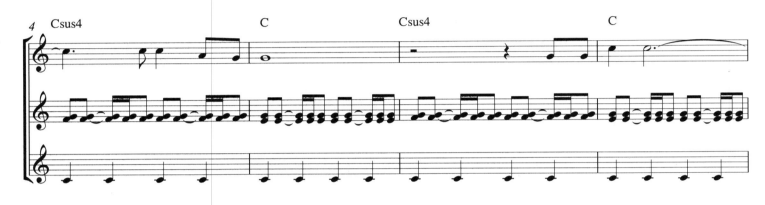

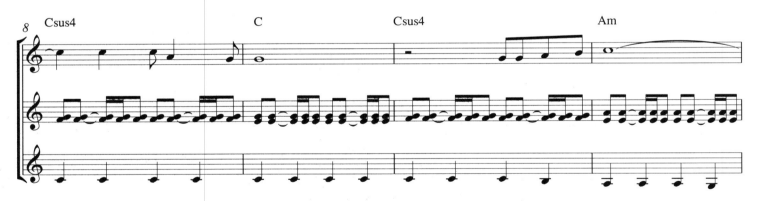

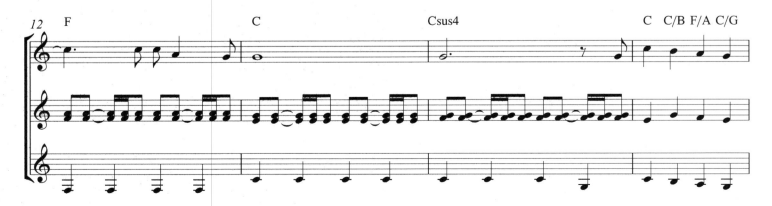

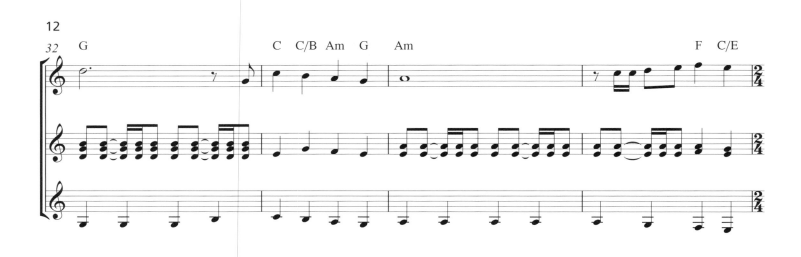

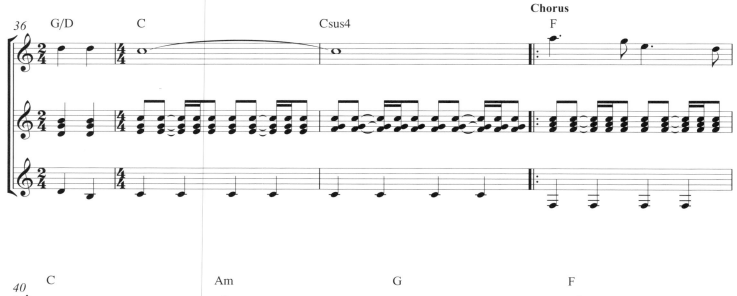

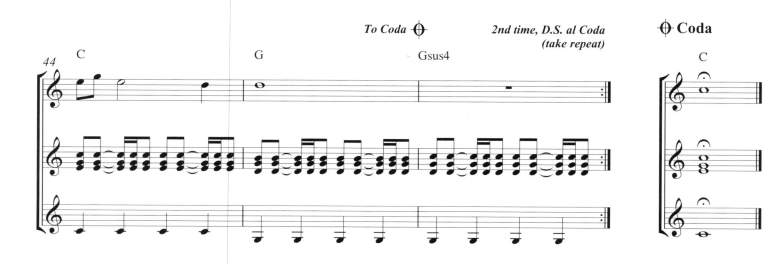

LET IT GO

from Disney's Animated Feature FROZEN

Music and Lyrics by Kristen Anderson-Lopez and Robert Lopez

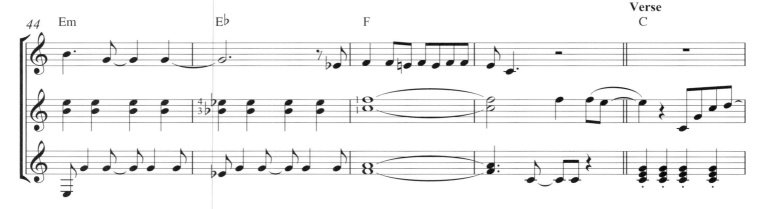

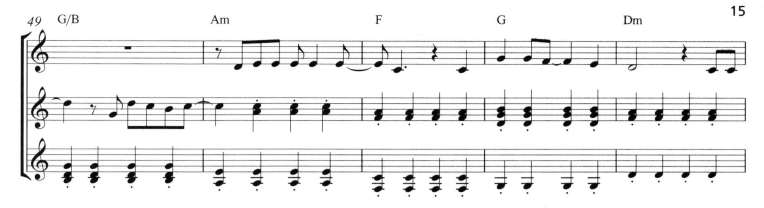

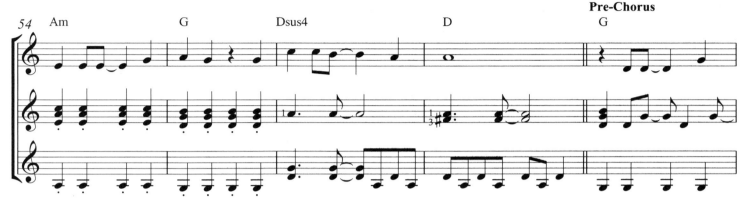

LET HER GO

Words and Music by Michael David Rosenberg

Chorus

To Coda ⊕

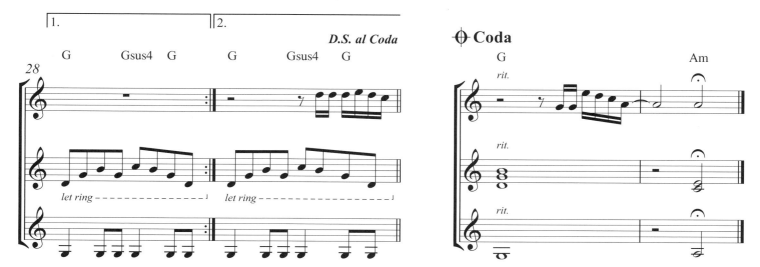

LOCKED OUT OF HEAVEN

Words and Music by Bruno Mars, Ari Levine and Philip Lawrence

Chorus

Interlude

To Coda ⊕   ***2nd time, D.S. al Coda***
                (take repeats)   ⊕ **Coda**

RADIOACTIVE

Words and Music by Daniel Reynolds, Benjamin McKee, Daniel Sermon, Alexander Grant and Josh Mosser

Intro
Moderately fast

Verse

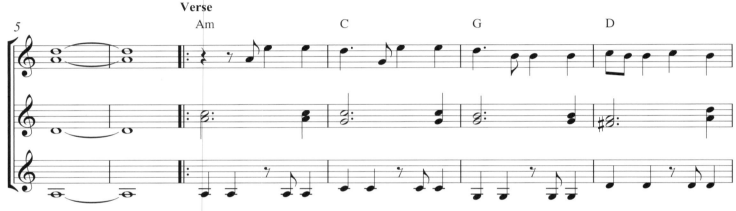

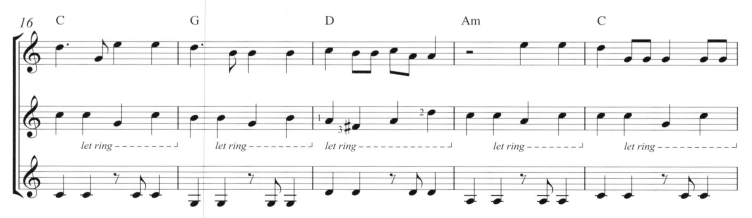

Pre-Chorus

Chorus

ROAR

Words and Music by Katy Perry, Lukasz Gottwald, Max Martin, Bonnie McKee and Henry Walter

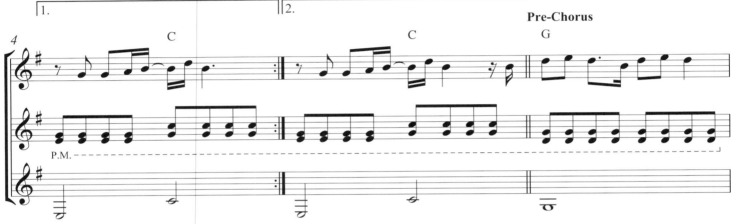

*Palm mute

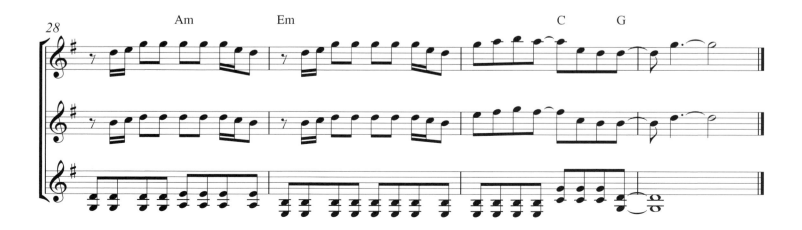

ROYALS

Words and Music by Ella Yelich-O'Connor and Joel Little

*Strum muted strings.

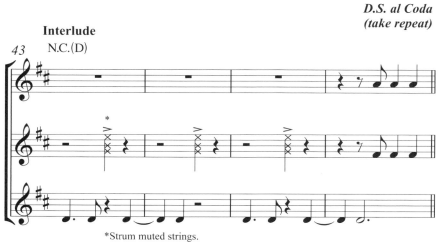

*Strum muted strings.

SAY SOMETHING

Words and Music by Ian Axel, Chad Vaccarino and Mike Campbell

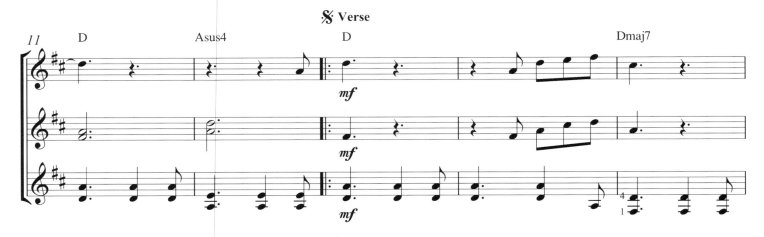

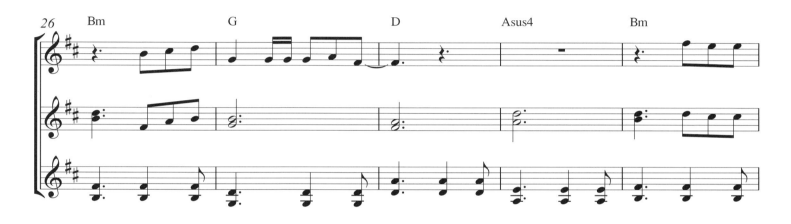

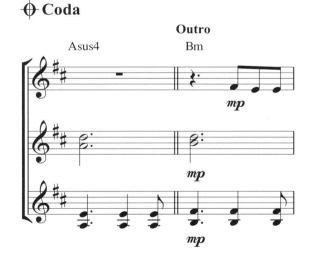

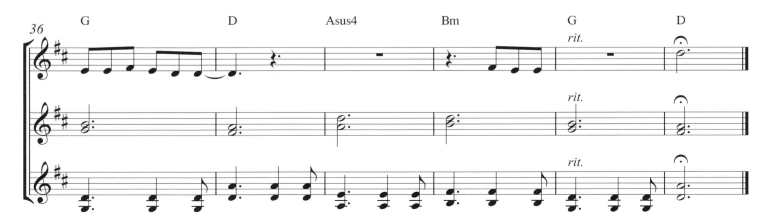

SKYFALL
from the Motion Picture SKYFALL
Words and Music by Adele Adkins and Paul Epworth

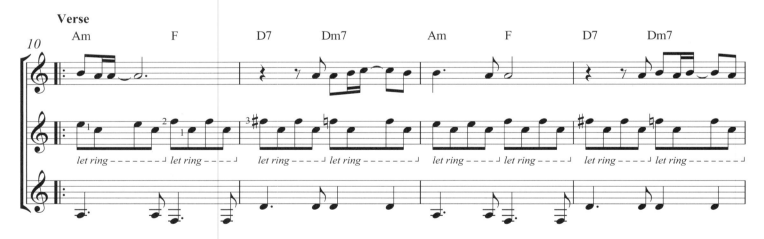

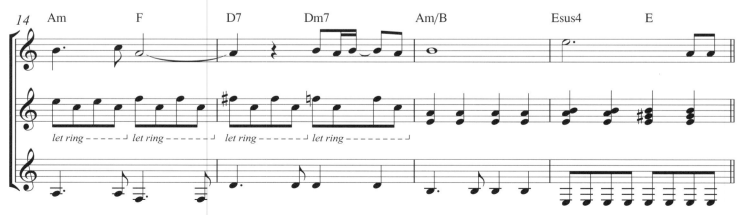

A THOUSAND YEARS

from the Summit Entertainment film THE TWILIGHT SAGA: BREAKING DAWN - Part 1

Words and Music by David Hodges and Christina Perri

Verse
Moderately

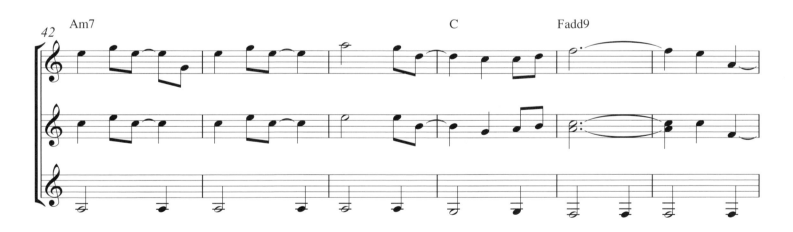

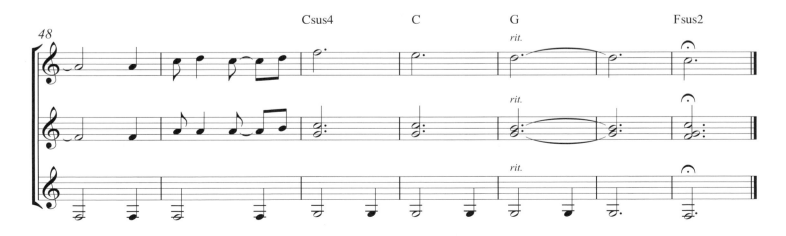

ESSENTIAL ELEMENTS FOR GUITAR, BOOK 1

INCLUDES TAB

Comprehensive Guitar Method
by Will Schmid and Bob Morris

Take your guitar teaching to a new level! With the time-tested classroom teaching methods of Will Schmid and Bob Morris, popular songs in a variety of styles, and quality demonstration and backing tracks on the accompanying CD, *Essential Elements for Guitar* is a staple of guitar teachers' instruction – and helps beginning guitar students off to a great start.

This method has been designed to meet the National Standards for Music Education, with features such as cross-curricular activities, quizzes, multicultural songs, basic improvisation and more. Concepts covered in Book 1 include: getting started; basic music theory; guitar chords; notes on each string; music history; ensemble playing; performance spotlights; and much more!

Songs used in Book 1 include such hits as: Dust in the Wind • Eleanor Rigby • Every Breath You Take • Hey Jude • Hound Dog • Let It Be • Ode to Joy • Rock Around the Clock • Stand by Me • Surfin' USA • Sweet Home Chicago • This Land Is Your Land • You Really Got Me • and more!

00862639 Book/CD Pack...$17.99

ESSENTIAL ELEMENTS FOR GUITAR, BOOK 2

Bob Morris

Essential Elements for Guitar, Book 2 is a continuation of the concepts and skills taught in Book 1 and includes all of its popular features as well – great songs in a variety of styles, a high-quality audio CD with demonstration and backing tracks, quizzes, music history, music theory, and much more. Concepts taught in Book 2 include: Playing melodically in positions up the neck; Playing movable chord shapes up the neck; Playing scales and extended chords in different keys; More right-hand studies – fingerpicking and pick style; Improvisation in positions up the neck; Studying different styles through great song selections; and more!

00865010 Book/CD Pack...$17.99

Essential Elements Guitar Ensembles

The songs in the Essential Elements Guitar Ensemble series are playable by three or more guitars. Each arrangement features the melody, a harmony part, and bass line in standard notation along with chord symbols. For groups with more than three or four guitars, the parts can be doubled. This series is perfect for classroom guitar ensembles or other group guitar settings.

THE BEATLES
00865008 Early Intermediate Level.....................$9.99

BOSSA NOVA
00865006 Intermediate/Advanced Level.............$9.99

CHRISTMAS CLASSICS
00865015 Mid-Intermediate Level $9.99

CHRISTMAS SONGS
00001136 Mid-Beginner Level............................$9.95

CLASSICAL THEMES
00865005 Late Beginner Level............................$9.99

DISNEY SONGS
00865014 Early Intermediate Level.....................$9.99

EASY POP SONGS
00865011 Mid-Beginner Level............................$9.99

DUKE ELLINGTON
00865009 Mid-Intermediate Level $9.99

GREAT THEMES
00865012 Mid-Intermediate Level $9.99

JIMI HENDRIX
00865013 Mid-Intermediate Level $9.99

JAZZ BALLADS
00865002 Early Intermediate Level.....................$9.99

JAZZ STANDARDS
00865007 Mid-Intermediate Level $9.99

POP HITS
00001128 Late Beginner Level............................$9.99

ROCK CLASSICS
00865001 Late Beginner Level............................$9.95

Flash Cards

96 CARDS FOR BEGINNING GUITAR
00865000...$7.95

Essential Elements Guitar Repertoire Series

Hal Leonard's Essential Elements Guitar Repertoire Series features great original guitar music based on a style or theme that is carefully graded and leveled for easy selection. The songs are presented in standard notation and tablature, and are fully demonstrated on the accompanying CD.

TURBO ROCK
Beginner Intermediate Level
by Mark Huls
00001076 Book/CD Pack $9.95

BLUES CRUISE
Mid-Intermediate Level
by Dave Rubin
00000470 Book/CD Pack $9.95

MYSTERIOSO
Mid-Intermediate Level
by Allan Jaffe
00000471 Book/CD Pack $9.95

DAILY GUITAR WARM-UPS

INCLUDES TAB

by Tom Kolb
Mid-Beginner to Late Intermediate
This book contains a wide variety of exercises to help get your hands in top playing shape. It addresses the basic elements of guitar warm-ups by category: stretches and pre-playing coordination exercises, picking exercises, right and left-hand synchronization, and rhythm guitar warm-ups.
00865004 Book/CD Pack $9.99

Essential Elements Guitar Songs

The books in the Essential Elements Guitar Songs series feature popular songs specially selected for the practice of specific guitar chord types. Each book includes eight great songs and a CD with fantastic sounding play-along tracks. Practice at any tempo with the included Amazing Slow Downer software!

POWER CHORD ROCK **INCLUDES TAB**
Mid-Beginner Level
00001139 Book/CD Pack $12.99

OPEN CHORD ROCK **INCLUDES TAB**
Mid-Beginner Level
00001138 Book/CD Pack $12.99

BARRE CHORD ROCK **INCLUDES TAB**
Late Beginner Level
00001137 Book/CD Pack $12.99

FOR MORE INFORMATION, SEE YOUR LOCAL MUSIC DEALER,
OR WRITE TO:

HAL•LEONARD® CORPORATION
7777 W. BLUEMOUND RD. P.O. BOX 13819 MILWAUKEE, WI 53213

Prices, contents, and availability subject to change without notice.